Everyday Inventions

Inventions We Use at

Home

Jane Bidder

GARETH**STEVENS**
GS
PUBLISHING
A Member of the WRC Media Family of Companies

Please visit our web site at: www.garethstevens.com
For a free color catalog describing Gareth Stevens Publishing's
list of high-quality books and multimedia programs,
call 1-800-542-2595 (USA) or 1-800-387-3178 (Canada).
Gareth Stevens Publishing's fax: (414) 332-3567.

Library of Congress Cataloging-in-Publication Data

Bidder, Jane.
    Inventions we use at home / by Jane Bidder.
      p. cm. — (Everyday inventions)
    Includes bibliographical references and index.
    ISBN-10: 0-8368-6898-6 — ISBN-13: 978-0-8368-6898-2 (lib. bdg.)
    1. Inventions—History—Juvenile literature.   2. Household appliances—
    Juvenile literature.   I. Title.
   T15.B54   2006
   643'.6—dc22   2006004289

This North American edition first published in 2007 by
Gareth Stevens Publishing
A Member of the WRC Media Family of Companies
330 West Olive Street, Suite 100
Milwaukee, WI 53212 USA

This U.S. edition copyright © 2007 by Gareth Stevens, Inc.
Original edition copyright © 2006 by Franklin Watts.
First published in Great Britain in 2006 by Franklin Watts,
338 Euston Road, London NW1 3BH, United Kingdom.

Watts series editor: Jennifer Schofield
Watts designer: Ross George
Watts picture research: Diana Morris

Gareth Stevens editors: Tea Benduhn and Barbara Kiely Miller
Gareth Stevens art direction: Tammy West
Gareth Stevens graphic designer: Dave Kowalski

Picture credits (t=top, b=bottom, l=left, r=right, c=center): British Museum/HIP/Topfoto: 22br. Peter
Connolly/AKG Images: 6bl. Randy Faris/CORBIS: 10t. Don Geyer/Alamy: 11t. Hutchison/Eye Ubiquitous: 10b.
Mary Evans Picture Library: 7. Museum of American History: 24bl. Nathan Norfolk: 16t. Picturepoint/Topham:
16b, 19c, 21 both. Steve Prezant/CORBIS: 24tr. Raytheon: 15. Science Museum/Science & Society Picture
Library: 26bl. Science Museum Pictorial/Science & Society Picture Library: 18bl. Science Picture Library: 25.
Victoria & Albert Museum, London/BAL: front cover cr, 8bl. Gary Vogelmann/Alamy: 6tr. Stephen Welstead/
CORBIS: 22tr.

Printed in the United States of America

1 2 3 4 5 6 7 8 9 10 09 08 07 06

Contents

Words that appear in the glossary are
printed in **boldface** type the first
time they occur in the text.

About Inventions

An invention is a **device** or a tool that is designed and made for the first time. The person who designs the device is called an inventor. This book looks at inventions that are found around the house. It also introduces inventors and shows how inventions we use at home have changed over time.

Easy Living

People have made many new items because they wanted to improve their lives. It is much easier, for example, to push a button on a washing machine than to spend hours washing clothes by hand. Inventions such as washing machines make life easier by saving time, and they have changed the way we live.

From One Comes Another

The final design of an invention is not always the same as the first. Many inventions change and improve over time. Clocks, for example, have become more accurate at keeping time than they were when cogs and springs moved the clock hands.

Accidentally Invented

Inventions are not always planned or are **developed** from other inventions. Sometimes, breakthroughs happen by accident. Dr. Percy Spencer was doing research on **radar**, in 1946, when he discovered that microwaves can cook food. One year later, a restaurant was using a microwave oven.

Toilets

When you use a toilet, you may not think of it as an amazing invention. Toilets, however, have not always been as **hygienic** and as comfortable as they are today. A long time ago, most people had to use a hole in the ground.

Friendly Chat

Nearly two thousand years ago, the Romans built rows of toilets that had a stream of water running beneath them. These toilets were in public bathhouses. People could sit on a toilet and talk to the person sitting next to them!

Potties for Adults

During the **Middle Ages**, wealthy people may have had toilets with water in the bowl, but most families could not afford such luxury. Many people, instead, used large containers, called chamber pots, which looked like training potties and had to be emptied after each use.

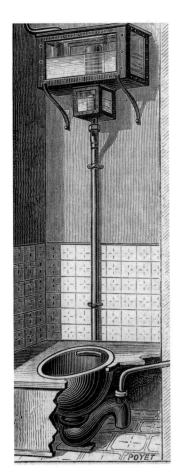

Modern Toilets

British inventor Alexander Cumming **patented** the first modern toilet in 1775. His toilet had a flushing device that sent waste out to newly built **sewers**. Cumming's toilet also had a **valve** and a curve in the pipe underneath the bowl. The curve kept water in the pipe, which kept sewer smells out of the house.

TIME LINE

2500 B.C.
People in Western India use a type of toilet inside their homes.

206 B.C.
People use toilets in the western Han Dynasty in China.

A.D. 100
The ancient Romans have toilets in their public baths.

1596
Sir John Harrington builds a flushing toilet for Queen Elizabeth I of England.

1775
Alexander Cumming patents a flushing device.

1889
European cities develop sewage treatment.

1981
NASA develops a waste management system for the Space Shuttle.

Locks and Keys

Locks and keys help people feel safe and keep **valuables** secure, but they are definitely not new inventions.

Fancy Locks and Keys from Long Ago

About four thousand years ago, the ancient Egyptians started to make locks and keys out of **iron**. Some of these had fancy designs and were pretty to look at.

Keys for Noblemen

By the Middle Ages, wealthy people in Europe had their family symbols and **coats of arms engraved** on their locks and keys. Master craftspeople made elaborate locks and keys to show off their metalwork skills. For daily use, however, on gates, chests, cupboards, and doors, they made simpler locks and keys.

Beating the Burglars

In 1851, Linus Yale Jr. of New York improved a design his father made in 1848 and patented a special bank lock. The "Yale Infallible Bank Lock," as he called it, was similar to many of the locks used today. His lock had an enclosed keyhole. Yale also developed a special flat key with jagged edges. The edges had to line up with metal pins inside the lock in order to turn and unlock.

Padlocks

In 1921, Harry Soref founded Master Lock in Milwaukee, Wisconsin. The company made make extra-strong padlocks with layers of **laminated** steel.

TIME LINE

2000 B.C.
Ancient Egyptians make iron and wooden locks and keys.

Middle Ages
Craftspeople make fancy keys for wealthy Europeans.

1600s
An unknown English inventor makes a keyless combination lock.

1873
James Sargent of New York creates the first lock that opens automatically at a designated time.

1920s
German-born, U.S. inventor Walter Schlage invents a push-button locking device for door knobs.

1980
Companies worldwide design digital keyless entry systems that use microchips to operate.

Toothbrushes

Today, many people have the good habit of brushing their teeth twice a day. Did you know that people were brushing their teeth as long ago as five thousand years?

Ancient Toothbrushes

Ancient Egyptians chewed the ends of **aromatic** sticks and rubbed their teeth with the frayed ends to clean their teeth.

Get Flossing!
Some scholars think that **prehistoric** humans may have used very thin twigs and stiff stems to floss their teeth.

Animal Hair

In 1498, the Chinese invented a toothbrush made of wild boar hairs attached to a handle made of bamboo or bone. Europeans used similar toothbrushes, but they had horsehair bristles.

Fantastic Plastic

In 1937, Wallace H. Carothers, at the DuPont company in the United States, invented nylon, which is a type of plastic. The next year, the DuPont company made nylon bristles for toothbrushes. Most toothbrush bristles since then have been made of nylon.

Clocks

From the moment their alarm clocks ring in the morning, people use clocks to make sure they are on time for school, work, trains, and buses. It took a while, however, before people were able to time their day like clockwork.

Sun Clocks

The ancient Egyptians built the first known clocks in about 3500 B.C. Their "Sun clocks" were tall, four-sided pillars that cast shadows on the ground according to the Sun's position. Unfortunately, because the clocks relied on sunlight, they worked only during daylight hours.

Tick Tock!
Clockwork is a mechanical way to power clocks. The hands move by means of gears pulled by weights or springs that slowly uncoil.

Mechanized Clocks

In 1656, Dutch scientist Christiaan Huygens made the first pendulum clock. A swinging pendulum moved a notched wheel that drove the clock's hands around. By 1675, Huygens had developed a wheel-and-spring assembly that is still used in some wind-up watches today.

pendulum

Using Crystals

In 1927, Canadian **engineer** Warren Marrison developed a clock that ran on **quartz crystals**. When an electric current passes through the crystal, it vibrates. The vibration causes the clock's regular ticking and accurate timekeeping.

TIME LINE

3500 B.C.
The Egyptians build Sun clocks to mark the time.

300 B.C.
The Greeks use water clocks.

A.D. 700
People make sand clocks to measure short periods of time.

Early 1300s
Italian cities build public clock towers with weight-driven timekeeping mechanisms.

1510
Peter Henlein invents the spring-powered clock in Germany.

1927
Marrison develops the quartz clock.

1950s
The National Institute of Standards and Time develops atomic clocks.

Microwave Ovens

Microwave ovens heat up or cook food much faster than ordinary ovens. Microwave ovens are a fairly recent invention that became popular very quickly — especially with people who are in a hurry or do not want to spend hours cooking.

Popping Mad!

In 1946, Dr. Percy Spencer discovered the power of microwaves to cook food. While researching radar equipment at Raytheon, in Massachusetts, a tube he was working with melted the candy bar in his pocket. He then wondered if the tube could be used to heat other foods. He put some popcorn kernels near the tube and they popped! Raytheon soon started making microwave ovens.

Giant Radarange

In 1947, Raytheon made the first microwave oven, the Radarange (*below, right*). The oven was nearly 6 feet (2 meters) tall — much bigger than microwave ovens today. Restaurants were the first to use the Radarange.

Today's Microwave Ovens

At first, many people did not want to use microwave ovens. They were afraid that **microwave energy** might be dangerous. By the 1970s, microwave technology improved, and microwave ovens had become **inexpensive** to buy, making them popular for home use.

TIME LINE

1946
Microwave energy melts Dr. Percy Spencer's candy bar. Spencer discovers that microwave energy can cook food.

1947
U.S. restaurants use the first microwave ovens.

1970s
People begin to use microwave ovens in their homes.

2000s
Most U.S. homes have microwave ovens.

More Than Ovens
Microwave energy is used for more than just ovens. It is also used in televisions, telephones, and in radar machines that detect the speeds of moving cars.

Lightbulbs

Today, it is hard to imagine homes, schools, and cities with no electric lights. Before 1809, however, people used candles and lanterns to find their way in the dark.

Before Lightbulbs

In 1809, English chemist Sir Humphry Davy discovered how to produce electric light. He connected two wires to a battery and a strip of charcoal, and the strip glowed. His invention, called arc lighting, was safe to use in mines because it would not catch fire.

Different Strengths
The strength of a lightbulb is measured in watts, named after Scottish inventor James Watt. The higher the wattage, the brighter the light.

The First Electric Lightbulbs

In 1875, Henry Woodward and Matthew Evans filed a patent in Canada for a lightbulb. They did not have enough money to develop their invention so Thomas Edison, of New Jersey, bought their patent. Edison improved their idea and, in 1879, made the first electric lightbulb.

How Do Bulbs Work?

Lightbulbs use electricity to heat a thin piece of metal wire, called a filament, so that it glows. Edison used **carbon** for the filament and put it inside a glass bulb. He vacuumed the air out of the bulb so the filament would not burn away. In 1906, the General Electric company replaced carbon filaments with **tungsten** because this metal lasted longer than carbon.

filament

TIME LINE

1809
Sir Humphry Davy invents arc lighting in England.

1860s
Joseph Swan works on making a lightbulb in England.

1927
German scientists design a fluorescent lamp.

1950s
General Electric develops halogen lightbulbs.

2000s
Scientists search for energy-efficient lighting, such as LED lights.

Vacuum Cleaners

Without vacuum cleaners, carpeted floors would be dusty and dirty. These machines use an air pump to pull dirt from the floor. The dirt collects in a bag or container that can be emptied.

On a Carpet

About 75 percent of the "dirt" on carpets is flakes of dead skin. The flakes end up on the floor with hair, mites, and other dirt.

Booth's Big Machines

British engineer H. Cecil Booth came up with the idea for an electric vacuum cleaner when he put a handkerchief over a chair and breathed in through it. When he saw the dust on the other side of the handkerchief, he got the idea for "Booth's cleaning pump." His huge machine cleaned floors by sucking up dirt.

Super Hoover

In Ohio, in 1906, James Spangler made a vacuum cleaner out of a fan, a box, a pillowcase to catch the dirt, and a **rotating** brush to sweep the carpet. Two years later, he sold his idea to William Hoover. The new vacuum cleaner sold so well that some people call the machine a "Hoover" instead of a vacuum cleaner.

Lighter and More Powerful

Not many families had vacuum cleaners before World War II because they were very expensive. After 1945, companies **mass produced** vacuum cleaners that were both lighter and less expensive, making them more popular.

TIME LINE

1869
Ives McAffey sells a hand-powered vacuum cleaner, the Whirlwind, in Chicago.

1901
British engineer H. Cecil Booth invents the first electric vacuum cleaner.

1906
James Spangler makes a smaller, easier-to-use vacuum cleaner.

1908
Spangler sells his idea to the Hoover Company. They launch the first vacuum cleaner with attachments and a cleaning bag.

2000
Several companies begin producing robotic floor cleaners such as Roomba, Robomaxx, Trilobite, and Floor Bot.

Washing Machines

Doing laundry has been easier since washing machines were invented. Instead of washing clothes by hand, people can clean them with the touch of a button or the turn of a dial.

Nonelectric Machines

In 1782, Henry Sidgier patented a washing device in England. His early washing machine looked like a cage with wooden rods for handles. People put their dirty clothes in the cage, sank the cage in a bucket of hot water, and turned the wooden rods to wash the clothes.

Talking Machines
Washing machines that talk to you are not far off. Perhaps they will say things such as "fill up with detergent" or "close the door."

Thundering Machines

In 1906, Alva J. Fisher designed an electric washing machine for the Hurley Machine Company in Chicago, Illinois. The machine had a small, uncovered motor attached to the side. Water could spill out onto the wires, giving the person using the machine an electric shock.

Twin Tubs

During the 1960s, companies started to make twin tub washing machines. The machines had two drums next to each other. One drum washed the clothes, then the clothes had to be put into the next drum to spin the water out. Today's machines have a single drum that washes and spins.

TIME LINE

1782
Henry Sidgier designs the first washing machine, in England.

1906
Alva J. Fisher designs an electric washing machine in Chicago, Illinois.

1937
Bendix Corporation **demonstrates** an automatic washing machine in Louisiana.

1950s
Companies in the United States and England start making washing machines that also dry clothes.

1960s
Twin tub washing machines are affordable for households.

1970s
Front loading washing machines start to become popular among people who want to save water.

Chairs

People sit on chairs every day. But have you ever wondered who invented the very first chair?

Chair Fact
The biggest chair in the world is in Manzano, Italy. It stands 65 feet (20 m) tall. That's about the height of a seven story building!

Egyptian Chairs

Chairs were used by Egyptian rulers as long ago as 5000 B.C. Wooden chairs with beautifully carved legs were found in the tombs of pharaohs.

Carved Chairs

Between A.D. 1300 and 1600, chairs stopped being a sign of privilege and wealth and became affordable for the general public. People covered chair seats with materials such as silk and velvet, which made them comfortable. Chairs then became very fashionable and showed the styles of the time.

Shaker Chairs

In the 1700s, members of the Shaker religious community began to make chairs in the United States. Their simple, undecorated, wooden chairs were sturdy, and soon people outside the community wanted them. Shaker chairs are still popular today.

5000 B.C.
Ancient Egyptians and Greeks have chairs.

Middle Ages
Chairs are a luxury, so many people sit on the ground or on stools.

1300s onward
Chairs become more affordable for the general public.

1600s
Chair seats are made of soft materials.

1700s onward
Shakers make chairs in the United States. All over the world, people make a variety of chairs to suit fashions.

1950s
Plastic makes chairs lighter in weight.

1960s
Designers make new forms of chairs, such as the butterfly, beanbag, and egg or pod chair.

Refrigerators

Have you ever noticed that if you do not keep certain foods, such as milk, in a refrigerator, they go bad? Long ago, there were no refrigerators. People stored food in an icebox to keep it cold and fresh.

The First Fridge

In 1851, Dr. John Gorrie was granted the first U.S. patent for an ice-making machine. He put water in a container and covered the container with **brine**. He then passed cold air through the brine. The brine remained liquid because it freezes at a lower temperature than pure water, but the cold brine chilled the water until it froze.

Ammonia Refrigerators

In France, in 1859, Ferdinand Carre further developed Gorrie's ice-making machine. Instead of using cold air to cool the liquid, he used **ammonia** gas. Ammonia is easier to chill to very low temperatures, so it is an even stronger **coolant**. Although Carre's machine worked very well, the ammonia gas was dangerous if it leaked.

Refrigerators at Home

In 1873, Carl von Linde developed the first practical refrigerator for companies to use. Other designers developed his ideas further, and more people started to buy refrigerators. In 1916, the Frigidaire Company in Indiana began making self-contained refrigerators that became a well-known household brand.

Other Inventions

People use many other inventions at home that are important in daily life.

Ironing Boards

In 1892, Sarah Boone invented an ironing board in Connecticut. She designed her board so that sleeves could be ironed easily.

Irons

Henry W. Seeley of New York invented an electric iron in 1882. His iron weighed almost 15 pounds (7 kilograms) and took a long time to warm up. By the 1950s, companies were making lighter irons with wooden handles (*left*). Today, irons are light and easy to use, and they heat up almost instantly.

Cutlery

Although people in the Middle East used forks as early as A.D. 600, people in Europe did not use them until the 1500s. The  Romans designed the first spoons with handles in the first century. After 1669, when King Louis XIV of France made pointed knives illegal to use at the dinner table, people ground down the tips of their knives and made rounded table knives. Today, forks, spoons, and knives come in many different styles.

Plates and Bowls

Some scholars think that the oldest pottery bowls were used in Japan in 10,000 B.C. Today, dishes are still made from pottery, but they are also made from glass, metal, wood, and plastic.

ELECTRICITY

Scientists have worked with electricity for hundreds of years. Many of the inventions in this book, however, would not have been possible without the discoveries of Alessandro Volta and Michael Faraday.

Italy's Alessandro Volta found that dipping a piece of copper and a piece of zinc in salt water produced an electric current. The combination of zinc-coated copper in salt water made the first electric cell. Volta then made a pile of these cells to make the first battery.

Michael Faraday, from England, discovered that electricity could make magnets turn in circles. Scientists used Faraday's discovery to create the electric motors that are found in many household inventions today.

Time Line

5000 B.C.
Ancient Egyptians and
Greeks have chairs.

3500 B.C.
Ancient Egyptians build Sun clocks.

3000 B.C.
Ancient Egyptians chew on pencil-
sized sticks to clean their teeth.

2500 B.C.
People use indoor toilets in India.

2000 B.C.
Ancient Egyptians make locks
and keys of iron and wood.

300 B.C.
The Greeks build water clocks.

A.D. 100
The ancient Romans have
toilets in their public baths.

Middle Ages
European craftspeople make fancy keys.

Early 1300s
Italian cities build public clock
towers with weight-driven
timekeeping mechanisms.

1510
Peter Henlein invents the spring-
powered clock in Germany.

1596
England's Sir John Harrington builds a
flushing toilet for Queen Elizabeth I.

1668
Police commissioner in Paris decrees
that all homes must have toilets.

1748
William Cullen demonstrates
artificially cooled air at the
University of Glasgow, Scotland.

1775
Alexander Cumming patents
a flushing device.

1780
William Addis mass produces
toothbrushes in England.

1782
Henry Sidgier designs the first
washing machine, in England.

1809
Sir Humphry Davy invents
arc lighting in England.

1851

Dr. John Gorrie patents an ice-making machine in Florida.

Linus Yale Jr. invents the Yale Infallible Bank Lock.

1869

Ives McAffey sells his hand-powered Whirlwind vacuum cleaner.

1879

Thomas Edison makes an electric lightbulb.

1906

James Spangler makes a small, easy-to-use vacuum cleaner.

Alva J. Fisher designs an electric washing machine in Chicago.

1916

Frigidaire becomes a popular brand of refrigerator.

1927

Marrison develops the quartz clock.

1938

DuPont makes nylon toothbrush bristles.

1946

Microwave energy melts Dr. Percy Spencer's candy bar and pops popcorn.

Companies begin to mass produce refrigerators.

1947

Restaurants use microwaves.

GE makes a two-door combination refrigerator-freezer.

1950s

The National Institute of Standards and Time develops atomic clocks.

GE develops halogen light bulbs.

Plastic makes chairs lightweight.

Washing machines also dry clothes.

1970s

People use microwaves at home.

Front loading washing machines become popular for saving water.

1980

Companies develop keyless entry systems that use microchips.

1981

NASA develops a waste management system for the space shuttle.

2000s

Companies make robotic floor cleaners, such as Roomba.

More than 99 percent of U.S. homes have refrigerators.

Nearly 95 percent of U.S. homes have microwave ovens.

Glossary

ammonia
a colorless gas that has a strong smell and has been used as a refrigerant

aromatic
having a strong, pleasant smell

brine
salty water

carbon
a natural solid substance found in coal

coats of arms
the special patterns or badges that represent a family or a country

coolant
a liquid used to make something cold

demonstrates
shows

developed
made something better

device
a piece of equipment designed to do a certain task

engineer
a scientist who studies, designs, and builds machines, buildings, or other objects

engraved
carved into metal, glass, wood, rock, plastic, or another hard surface

hygienic
clean and germ-free

inexpensive
does not cost a lot of money

iron
a hard, silvery gray metal

laminated
made of layers of materials that are firmly attached to each other

mass produced
made many copies of the same item, usually with the help of machines

microwave energy
very short waves of electricity that can be used as power

Middle Ages
the period in history from about A.D. 900 until the late 1400s

patented
claimed the ownership rights to an invention so it cannot be copied by others

prehistoric
the time long before written history

quartz crystals
shiny stones that are formed
from the mineral quartz

radar
an electronic device that sends
radio waves and measures the
waves when they bounce back

rotating
turning or spinning around
in a full circle

sewers
systems of pipes that carry away
waste from toilets

tungsten
a metal that does not melt easily

valuables
items that are worth a lot of money

valve
an opening in a pipe that allows
water to go in or out of the pipe

Further Information

Books

It's About Time! Science Projects: How Long Does It Take?
Sensational Science Experiments (series).
Robert Gardner (Enslow)

The Science of a Light Bulb. Science World (series).
Neville Evans (Raintree)

Web Sites

U.S. Patent and Trademark office Kids' pages
www.hfmgv.org/collections/collections/toys.asp

Smithsonian National Museum of American History: Edison Invents!
invention.smithsonian.org/centerpieces/edison/

Publisher's note to educators and parents: Our editors have carefully reviewed these
Web sites to ensure that they are suitable for children. Many Web sites change frequently,
however, and we cannot guarantee that a site's future contents will continue to meet our
high standards of quality and educational value. Be advised that children should be closely
supervised whenever they access the Internet.

Index